2gether

Do-N-Poetry with God is Poetic

Inspirational Poems

BY A MAN AND WOMAN OF GOD

Calvin & Anita Boone

2GETHER: DO-N-POETRY WITH GOD IS POETIC

Copyright © 2020 by Calvin & Anita Boone

All rights reserved. No part of this book may be reproduced or transmitted in any form or by any means without written permission from the author.

ISBN: 978-1-7358359-3-8
Library of Congress Control Number: 2021912755

Printed in the USA by The Vision to Fruition Publishing House (www.vtfpublishing.com)

Psalm 91 (KJV)

¹ He that dwelleth in the secret place of the most High shall abide under the shadow of the Almighty.

² I will say of the LORD, He is my refuge and my fortress: my God; in Him will I trust.

³ Surely, He shall deliver thee from the snare of the fowler, and from the noisome pestilence.

⁴ He shall cover thee with His feathers, and under His wings shalt thou trust: His truth shall be thy shield and buckler.

⁵ Thou shalt not be afraid for the terror by night; nor for the arrow that flieth by day;

⁶ Nor for the pestilence that walketh in darkness; nor for the destruction that wasteth at noonday.

⁷ A thousand shall fall at thy side, and ten thousand at thy right hand; but it shall not come nigh thee.

⁸ Only with thine eyes shalt thou behold and see the reward of the wicked.

⁹ Because thou hast made the LORD, which is my refuge, even the most High, thy habitation;

¹⁰ There shall no evil befall thee, neither shall any plague come nigh thy dwelling.

¹¹ *For He shall give His angels charge over thee, to keep thee in all thy ways.*

¹² *They shall bear thee up in their hands, lest thou dash thy foot against a stone.*

¹³ *Thou shalt tread upon the lion and adder: the young lion and the dragon shalt thou trample under feet.*

¹⁴ *Because He hath set His love upon me, therefore will I deliver him: I will set Him on high, because He hath known my name.*

¹⁵ *He shall call upon me, and I will answer Him: I will be with Him in trouble; I will deliver him, and honor him.*

¹⁶ *With long life will I satisfy Him, and shew Him my salvation.*

In Memory Of

GENEVA GATLING BOONE

JANET BOONE

THOMAS U. TAYLOR
UNITED STATES ARMY VETERAN (WW II)

ROY TAYLOR
(UNITED STATES ARMY VETERAN)

GREGORY TAYLOR
UNITED STATES ARMY VETERAN (VIETNAM)

ALFRED AND JUANITA AUGUSTUS

WENDELL AND CASSIE DEAS

ALICE COLEMAN JACKSON

ROXSAN RODRIGUEZ

In Loving Memory

THOSE WE *love* DON'T GO AWAY
THEY WALK BESIDE US EVERYDAY.
UNSEEN, UNHEARD BUT *always* NEAR
STILL LOVED, STILL MISSED AND VERY DEAR.

Table of Contents

Introduction
2gether: Do-N-Poetry with God is Poetic 10

Inspirational Poems by Calvin Boone 13
Glad I Took the Time to Sit Down and Talk 15
After Waking Up, Get Ready to Face Up to God 18
Family is Important and Necessary 21
Reasons We Call on Jesus, But Know U Can Call Him Anytime 24
In Battle God Knows Where You Are 27
When God's People are in a Fight (Coronavirus) 30
God Had Jesus Set the Table; How Many are Eating the Food? 34
Why Can't We Come Together and Get on the Same Page? 37
Judge; Not the Outside; But Inside a Person's Heart & Blood 40
Looking for a Leader and It's Not That Man 43
No Man is Greater than God 47
Disappointed for a Day 51
Say Hey! I Think We All Need to Pray 55
Giving Back Pushes Us Forward 59
Covid-19 but What About a God Who is Our King 62
There Is Something (Beautiful) About a Day that God Made 65

Inspirational Poems by Anita Boone 69
Jehovah Elohim, Our Creator 72
Morning Sunrise 74
Did You Say Your Prayers Today? 76
Forgiving One Another 78
God Loves a Cheerful Giver 80
Keep Your Eyes on the Prize 82
I Love My Husband 84
Let No Man Put Asunder 86

Thank You, Mom 88
While Waiting Patiently for God 90
God Always Has a Ram in the Bush 92
My Sheep Hear My Voice 94
Who Do You Say That I Am? 96
God Answers Prayers 98
Spiritual Gift of Wisdom 101
Victory in Jesus 103
Nobody Knows the Day or Hour 105
Don't Wait for Tomorrow 107
Joy Cometh in the Morning 109

Testimonies *112*
About Calvin Boone 124
Calvin's Acknowledgments 126
About Anita Boone 128
Anita's Acknowledgments 130
About the Publisher 133

Introduction

The title of our book *2gether: Do-N-Poetry with God is Poetic* is based on inspirational poems about life's experiences, spiritual truths, and revelations received from God. Both my wife and I were inspired to write this book of poems for God has blessed and healed us through prayer for such a time as this where God's people are experiencing COVID-19, Black Lives Matter issues, and violence in the world.

Our book title came to us because we realized that God has given us the talent to write inspirational poems and that He is poetic about how He goes about doing things that not only blesses us but others who are going through.

This year has been a test of our faith with all the issues going on, but He gives us the Bible and other inspirational materials to read to help us. This is the time like never before where families need to be closer to God and each other. It is a time to be thankful just to wake up in the morning and sing songs of praises to the Almighty God!

Jesus said in John 16:33 (KJV) – *"These things I have spoken unto you, that in Me ye might have peace. In the world ye shall have tribulation: but be of good cheer, I have overcome the world."*

We hope and pray that you, your family, and friends will enjoy reading our book of inspirational poems and that they will bring comfort to you.

To God Be the Glory!

2gether:
Do-N-Poetry with God
is Poetic

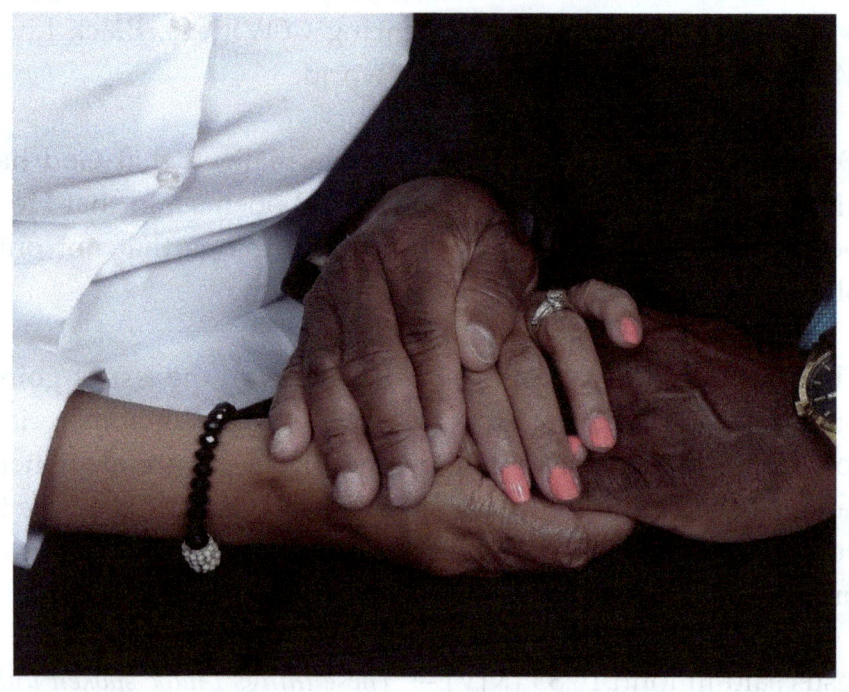

2Gether: Do-N-Poetry with God is Poetic

2gether Do-N-Poetry with God is Poetic
Because from the beginning to the end of each poem,
You feel in your heart, there are things He wants to say to you,
and He needs you to get it,
So, information on life issues can be shared,
And by using poetry, He took the time and
we know that He cared.

Working with God, we know He saved our marriage,
And we needed prayer and faith in the times of trouble.
There are poems that touched our heart,
and we believe His heart as well,
and after reading them, please go and tell how
He needs us to pray and eat His food,
get along with each other and tell the Good News.

There is nothing that God can't do.
He brings everything and everyone together
And He did it for us too!
Now don't you forget it, because God is very poetic!

To God be the Glory!

Your Thoughts

INSPIRATIONAL POEMS

By Calvin Boone

Dedication

First of all, I dedicate this book to the Father, Son and the Holy Spirit. For without the anointing, *2gether: Do-N-Poetry with God is Poetic* would not have been written.

I dedicate this book of poems to our Pastors/Apostles Tony and Cynthia Brazelton, our spiritual Dad and Mom. I thank God for their prayers for our marriage and family. God hears and answers prayers. May God continue to bless you and your family.

To my loving mother, Geneva Gatling Boone (deceased) and my sister, Janet Boone (deceased), thank you for always loving and supporting me.

To my two daughters, Tonia and Stacy; and four grandkids: Princess, PJ, Alex and JR, and to all my brothers. I love you.

To my church family and all my friends and anyone who chooses to read *2gether: Do-N-Poetry with God is Poetic*, my prayer and hope is that you will be inspired to do great things together to make a difference in this world. May God bless you all, and anyone that I have not mentioned who were instrumental in helping me accomplish the work of God.

To God Be the Glory!

Glad I Took the Time to Sit Down and Talk

Glad I Took Time to Sit Down and Talk

Just the other day after finishing my walk,
I was reminded of the time when you wanted me to sit down and talk.
Every time I saw you, I'd quicken my walk,
Not knowing why, but I didn't want to talk.
I thank God for your participation in having me to sit down and have a conversation.

This conversation, God, my Pastors and prayers of the righteous were important in saving our marriage,
And helped to reveal the enemy who had me in such a big hurry.
I am glad God opened my eyes to see,
That by slowing down, my wife was still there, waiting for me.

Nugget: It pays to slow down and have the sight that God gave you, so you will not miss out on what He has and still wants for you.

Proverbs 16:9 (NKJV) *A man's heart plans His way, But the Lord directs His steps.*

To God Be the Glory!!!

Your Thoughts

After Waking Up, Get Ready to Face Up to God

After Waking Up Get Ready to Face Up to God

After waking up, get ready to face up to God
And if you give this serious thought,
It should be something that is pleasing,
Rewarding and not that hard.
Try thanking Him for all the things He has done
For you in your life,
And all the times He could have been hard,
But showed love, compassion and was nice.

So, remember while you have the opportunity,
And are blessed to wake up.
I know there are so many things you want to share with Him now,
That you have gotten yourself ready to face up.
For God loves it when you face up to Him and don't run away,
And that means you are in the position He wanted for you and that is the position to pray.

Nugget: Remember, after waking up get ready to face up to God and thank Him for where He has brought you and me which is a mighty long way. Know that we did not and could not have done it by ourselves.

Psalm: 124:2 *If it had not been for the Lord who was on our side, when men rose up against us.*

To God Be the Glory!!!

Your Thoughts

Family is Important and Necessary

Family is Important and Necessary

Family is Important and so very Necessary.
So is a mother's child and their baby carriage.
We are God's family and this is how He created it to be.
For sometimes our problems may become heavy, you see?
But through prayer, God becomes that carriage for you and me.

We are not perfect; may fall short of the person He needs us to be,
Yet He still sees us as Family and Necessary.
I know I will always love family and pray they love me,
For God has placed this in my heart so I can remain free.

Forgive your Family member if they make a mistake,
And pray for them, because that's what it takes.
So, pray for your father, pray for your mother, pray for your sister and pray for your brother.
And oh, by the way, pray for yourself as well for we all make mistakes, only time tells.

But because of the love of God, He never left the children of Israel and He won't leave us, ok?
So, don't you think He expects this from Families today?
Keep in mind that Family is Important and Necessary
And if ever we need help, God is our supported baby carriage.

To God Be the Glory!

Your Thoughts

Reasons We Call on Jesus, But Know U Can Call Him Anytime

Reasons We Call on Jesus, But Know U Can Call Him Anytime

Reasons - I'm having some troubles in my marriage and it looks like we may break up. I need help to encourage me not to give up – Call on Jesus!

Reasons - My children are out of order; they don't want to listen and are a little too much and I can no longer tap them on their butts - Call on Jesus!

Reasons - My family and friends don't want to talk or see me anymore and when I call or go by their house, some of them won't let me in the door - Call on Jesus!

Reasons - I'm having problems on my job with my boss making it hard for me to get my pay grade. I've done everything I can do to show that I am a good employee and well behaved - Call on Jesus!

Reasons - I'm having sickness and pain in my body and the doctors are saying that I won't get well and I've even heard some of my family members say only time will tell – Call on Jesus!

Reasons – I'm in prison and I did not do the crime, I've been in this jail for such a long time. I didn't know you Jesus when they accused me of this crime but have gotten to know You and what a better time to – Call on Jesus!

Your Thoughts

In Battle God Knows Where You Are

In Battle God Knows Where You Are

You may be in a fight and it could be at night.
But don't you worry because God sees your light.
Remember a fight can come anytime, don't have to be at night.

But having God on your side, keeps you unafraid,
And ready for the big knockout.
So, go ahead, lift up your hands and raise them to God,
Giving Him the glory for your loving but fighting heart.

The heart to fight and the heart to win,
Knowing if you repent, He has forgiven all your sins
So, in battle God knows where you are
And He will never lose sight that you are His child which
Makes you part of His marvelous light.

Nugget: Remember, we all have battles in life like marriage problems, friendship problems, health challenges, homelessness, wrongfully incarcerated, mental health issues, being bullied or unemployment. Just remember by praying and having faith in God, He has already defeated these battles for you and me.

2 Chronicles 20:15 (KJV) *And He said, Hearken ye, all Judah, and ye inhabitants of Jerusalem, and thou King Jehoshaphat, Thus saith the Lord unto you, Be not afraid nor dismayed by reason of this great multitude; for the battle is not yours, but God's.*

To God Be the Glory!

Your Thoughts

When God's People are in a Fight (Coronavirus)

When God's People are in a Fight (Coronavirus)

When God's people are in a fight,
His Son Jesus always shines His marvelous light.
It's not like all of a sudden, He leaves us by saying, good night.
No, He is right there with us in the fight.
When a well named boxer trains for a major fight,
Everyone is there to see if he trained just right.

Well Jesus gave us prayer and scripture to knock Coronavirus out.
He said in His word that He would never leave nor forsake us but that He would be with us always even until the end of time.
So, I pray we all keep this in mind,
The battle is not ours says the Lord.
I also pray we will have the faith to believe that we can count it all joy.

Now Jesus loves us so much, He has reset the time.
Time at home, time alone, time to pray,
And time to realize Jesus has us doing things a different way.
He wants us to know that in Isaiah 54:17, *No weapon that is formed against us shall prosper; and every tongue that shall rise against us in judgment will be condemned, in the mighty name of Jesus.*

Remember Jesus has already won the coronavirus fight, but He needs us to be prepared for any upcoming fights.
Remember, He said in Romans 8:31 (KJV) – *If God be for us, who can be against us?*

I pray for and know that it is not easy for families who have loved ones sick and have lost someone in this fight.
Knowing you wanted to see them, but the situation was not right.

Even if you couldn't talk with them on the phone,
Know that God has never left and will never leave them alone.

Remember John 3:16 (KJV) says: *For God so loved the world, that He gave His only begotten Son, that whosoever believeth in Him should not perish, but have everlasting life.*

I thank God for the love He has for all of us and pray Psalm 91:10 over our lives. *There shall no evil befall thee, neither shall any plague come nigh thy dwelling.*

In the name of Jesus. Amen

To God be the Glory!

Your Thoughts

God had Jesus Set the Table; How Many are Eating the Food?

God had Jesus Set the Table; How Many are Eating the Food?

Just imagine a table being set by God's son, Jesus.
I know the table, chairs, napkins and tablecloth are like no other.

The silverware and chinaware are far better than our mothers.
Keep in mind His food is like no other
That He took the time to invite your father, mother
Sister, and brother.

He is mindful that He brought in more chairs
So, no one would be standing and therefore He invited
Your entire family
Now comes the food that He has prepared for us to eat.
Food that smells so good, it wakes you up from your sleep.
Food that nourishes our bodies and keep us from getting sick.
Now all we have to do is receive it.

Remember God had Jesus set the table,
Now, how many of us are eating the food?
I heard that He is serving us today,
The "in the beginning" meal which is Genesis.

Nugget: There is no food better than the food God had His Son, Jesus prepared for us to eat. I pray we say our grace and eat it. Bless the hands that prepared this food. Bless the life that was sacrificed. We pray this food to nourish our bodies so we'll have the strength to live as You would have us live.
Amen

Thank you, God. To God be the Glory!

Your Thoughts

Why Can't We Come Together and Get on the Same Page?

Why Can't We Come Together and Get on the Same Page?

I feel the reason we can't come together and get on the same page is because some of us are not well behaved.
We see Black. We see White. We see Brown and We see Red.
We see Racism which the enemy has deeply embedded in our heads which causes prejudice and discrimination,
Which happens all across this nation.
Directed against someone of a different race based on the belief that one's own race is superior,
Thereby causing another race to feel inferior.

God is the answer in getting us to come together and get on the same page.
He wants all of us to have love in our hearts and get saved!
If we as adults still have a problem with race today,
Take a close look at little children of all races at play,
They come together, they get on the same page, they get along with each other and they don't see race unless someone has educated them the wrong way.

Nugget: Don't focus on race and dividing God's people but focus on uniting them.

Matthew 18:1-2-3 (KJV) *At the same time came the disciples unto Jesus saying, who is the greatest in the Kingdom of Heaven? (2) And Jesus called a little child unto him, and set Him in the midst of them, (3) And said, Verily I say unto you, except ye be converted, and become as little children, ye shall not enter into the Kingdom of Heaven.*

Your Thoughts

Judge; Not Outside but Inside; a Person by Their Heart & Blood

Don't judge a person by their color

Judge Not Outside but Inside a Person by their Heart & Blood

I am Black and you are White
And you are Brown and you are Red
But if we all get sick, lying on an operating room bed
Jesus reminded me if the doctor has to go in
We all bleed the Blood Color Red
So try to remember to walk in Love
For we never know when we may need each other's Blood

For you see, we all are united by the Blood of Jesus
That He shed on the cross, saving us from being lost
So, if ever you choose to Judge someone by their Race
Remember, it was Jesus who allowed us all to take our place

Note that Color does not make us but if we are not careful, it could break us
Therefore, walk in Love and be careful how you Judge!

To God Be the Glory!

Nugget: Note, it is far more important to Judge a person by their Heart and Blood than by their Race. Appearances can sometime fool you but I pray you have the Heart and Blood of Jesus so He can lead you.

Matthew 7:1 *Judge not, that ye be not judged.*

Your Thoughts

Looking for a Leader and It's Not That Man

Looking for a Leader and It's not That Man

When looking for a leader, I believe God wants us to know that it is not that Man who will try and lead His people by His own hands without seeking Him, asking what are His plans?

Yes, Man was created in God's image, so He is a part of God's plan,
But when Man gets in trouble and needs help, I pray He understands that God is our leader, therefore seek God before seeking himself (Man).

When Man fell in the garden and some people are still trying to understand
Why it has been so difficult for some of His people and that Man.

Let us take a look at the original plan,
God has always been our leader, but the world keeps looking to Man.
Therefore, I pray to God we will all understand,
That He is our Leader who has given us the Bible to seek things we don't quite understand
Like, why we should seek Him first, and not that Man.

Matthew 6:33 (KJV) *But seek ye first the kingdom of God and His righteousness; and all these things shall be added unto you.*

John 15:4-6 (KJV) *Abide in me, and I in you. As the branch cannot bear fruit of itself, except it abide in the vine; no more can ye, except ye abide in me. I am the vine, ye are the branches: He that abideth in me, and I in him, the same bringeth forth much fruit: for without me ye can do nothing. If a man abide not in me, He is cast forth as a branch, and is withered; and men gather them, and cast them into the fire, and they are burned.*

Your Thoughts

No Man is Greater Than God

No Man is Greater than God

Being God for man is Hard,
Because He is constantly dealing with issues of the heart
This is no problem for God because He created man
and included His heart.
But for man to partake of God's loving heart,
We need to step it up and do our part.

Like being the man that God called us to be,
Leading by example and opening the eyes
So the Blind will see
God wants us to do this by stopping lying
But telling the truth about things
Stop killing each other and lifting your brother up as a king.
Stop seeing Color but loving and helping your brothers from different mothers.

Remember that Jesus asked His disciple, Simon Peter, three times, "Simon, do you love me?"
And Peter said, "You know that I love You."
Jesus said, "Then feed my sheep."
How can we as Men do this if we are constantly falling asleep?
Know that no Man is greater than God,
But we can be Great in Him if we allow Him to be Great in us.
We can start by walking in love and having a loving heart.

To God Be the Glory!!!

Romans 8:19 (KJV) *For the earnest expectation of the creature waiteth for the manifestation of the sons of God.*

Nugget: Remember Men, when you see a man on the ground, lift him up, don't push him back down, for that same man may one day help you out but he can't do it lying on the ground. Just think if that man is JESUS.

Your Thoughts

Disappointed for a Day

Disappointed for a Day

I remember when I was young,
And became disappointed for a day,
but God didn't want me to stay that way.
So, He told me to go back out and play
Because He realized this was the place
the enemy wanted me to stay.

Remember when we were kids
and we would mess up?
Causing our parents to tap us on our butts
We didn't like it so we would say,
you'll be sorry because I am going to run away.

But God kept us so close to home having
Mom cook our favorite meal
so, we didn't feel alone.
and after savoring His sweet smell,
we came running back home.

We learned our lesson, listening to dad, mom,
and what God had to say.
Like, it is important to know,
you may be disappointed for a day.
But God doesn't want you to stay that way.
So, get back out and play,
Freeing you up for He has so much more for you to do and say.

Nugget: We need to learn from our lessons and move forward not letting the enemy get us down, stealing our joy. Note, in

John 10:10 the enemy came but to steal, kill and destroy but God came that we may have life and have it more abundantly.

Your Thoughts

Say Hey! I Think We All Need to Pray

Say Hey! I Think We All Need to Pray

In a world like we are living in today,
We should all look at our family, neighbors, friends
and Say Hey! I think we all need to pray!
And I feel all should know what I mean,
Because the enemy has hit us hard with Covid-19

But if all of God's people come together
Praying on one accord,
Such things like this, I feel we could avoid.
For it is written that we are one nation under God,
But until we as God's people start living right,
Being it makes it hard.

We are also living in a world where we all should know
that All Lives Matter but because of the constant
mistreatment of the Black, Brown and Red race of
people, Casts a Huge Shadow
that it needs to be written in large letters on signs,
posters, and in the Streets that Black Lives Matter.

Through prayer, I'm beginning to see a change.
All of God's people marching under the same name.
This brings me back to the point where I want people to
realize it is important and to do what they Say
Like Hey, I think we all need to pray!

To God Be the Glory!

Nugget: We all need to keep in mind and never forget,
Prayer changes things and that is why we should not quit.

Luke 6:27-28 *But I say to you who hear, love your enemies, do good to those who hate you, Bless those who curse you pray for those who abuse you.*

Your Thoughts

Giving Back Pushes Us Forward

Giving Back Pushes Us Forward

Please don't forget to give back because it pushes
us forward in reflecting who God created in His image,
Giving back can help to uplift a people in need.
Therefore, we are not left standing watching someone
else's situation but helping through our own participation.

Remember giving back comes from the heart
and it is important that we do our part.
I often hear people who were once poor
but are now financially secure,
Say, I once lived in that neighborhood
and I don't want to forget where I came from.
So, I give back making sure I will help someone.

I pray they go deeper in their thinking and are mindful
of our creator (God) and His son, Jesus Christ who paid
the price which allows all of us to be able to give back
and giving back should be a part of our life.

Your Thoughts

Covid-19 but What About a God Who is Our King

Many people are talking about the virus Covid-19.
So many to the point, makes you wonder are we dishonoring Our God, our King?
Need I remind you that this virus is the enemy who is very mean.
He has stolen the lives of our friends and loved ones, so it seems.
But I know a God who is loving, caring and a restorer of dreams.
He has already received our friends and loved ones in heaven because He is King of Kings.

I know losing a loved one is not easy and can be a bit much,
But God comforts us in His loving arms with His marvelous and wonderful touch.
He is in charge and has the whole world in His hands
and wants us to know that life on earth will never be the same,
But know that we will get through this by seeking Him and calling on His Holy name.

I pray we will all realize that Covid-19 was such a bad dream,
until we woke up and started celebrating God
and His son Jesus Christ our true and Mighty King!

John 3:16 (KJV) *For God so loved the world, that He gave His only begotten Son, that whosoever believeth in Him should not perish, but have everlasting life.*

Nugget: Don't focus on the problem, focus on the problem solver, Jesus Christ.

Your Thoughts

There is Something (Beautiful) About a Day that God Made

There is Something (Beautiful) About a Day that God Made

There is something (Beautiful) about a day that God made
We see beauty all around us because He made it that way.
We see sooo many little children running around having fun and why?
Because God blessed them (Adam and Eve) and said to them, *"Be fruitful and multiply."*

We see Beautiful flowers blooming around this world each day.
Not only in flowers but in His people too, ok!
Everything He created speaks to us in a certain way

Because everything has a voice and something to say.
If we take the time to see the good He made, not the evil that is going on today.

For God created man and spoke a parable that he always ought to pray and not faint.

For this, I pray we all give thanks that by praying, it will change what we are seeing, hearing and noticing on today.

Like, There is something (Beautiful) about a day that God has made!

Genesis 1:28 (KJV) *And God blessed them, and God said unto them, Be fruitful and multiply.*

Luke 18:1 (KJV) *And He spake a parable unto them to this end, that men ought always to pray, and not to faint.*

Your Thoughts

INSPIRATIONAL POEMS

By Anita L. Boone

Dedication

This book is dedicated to the Father, Son and the Holy Spirit for blessing us to write a book of inspirational poems together as husband and wife.

I dedicate this book of poems to our Pastors/Apostles Tony and Cynthia Brazelton. I thank you for your prayers for our marriage and family. May God continue to bless you and your family.

To my loving parents, Thomas Taylor (deceased) and Virginia Taylor for always loving and supporting me, and for raising me up to become who I am in Christ Jesus.

To my brother, Pastor Thomas G. Taylor and His wife, Ruth Taylor and my two nephews, Girard and Lamone and my cousins, Cassandra, Nathan, Roxsan (deceased), Kevin, Bonnie, Shirley, Roland, Denise, and all my cousins, nieces, nephews, aunts and uncles, thank you for all of your love and support.

To my two bonus daughters, Tonia and Stacy; and four grandkids: Princess, PJ, Alex and JR. I love you all.

To my church family and all my friends and anyone who chooses to read *2gether Do-N-Poetry with God is Poetic*, my prayers and hope are that you will be inspired to do great things together to make a difference in this world. May God bless you all, and anyone that I have not mentioned who were instrumental in helping me throughout my life, thank you.

Christ in you, the hope of glory.
Colossians 1:27 (KJV)

Jehovah Elohim, Our Creator

Jehovah Elohim, Our Creator

You are the Creator of heaven and earth from the beginning.
You are the reason why we live and have our own being.
You are Jehovah Elohim, Our Creator and You made us
in Your image and likeness
And You showered us with Your love and kindness.

You blessed us with Your tender love and shield us from
danger every day,
And you help us through life's journey along the way.
You turn our darkness into light and can make a way out of
no way.
You are our Protector and you hear us when we pray.

For You are Lord of Lords and King of Kings,
And You are our Prince of Peace over the earth and all things.
You are always ready to fight our battles and to defend,
But most of all you are always with us even to the end.

Genesis 1:27 (KJV) *So God created man in His own image, in the image of God created He him; male and female created He them.*

Morning Sunrise

Morning Sunrise

I like to see the morning sunrise
Reach high into the pure blue skies
Beneath the soft white clouds above
Appears a beautiful rainbow of God's love

I like to hear the birds when they sing in the trees
And to feel the soft cool gentle breeze
Makes me laugh and smile along the way
And give thanks to God for waking me up to see
another new day

But most of all, I thank God for His precious
Son, Jesus
He loved us so much that He died on the cross for us
And I will rejoice and praise our Heavenly Father
Because He is the same yesterday, today and forever.

Lamentations 3:22-23 (GNT) *The Lord's unfailing love and mercy still continue. Fresh as the morning, as sure as the sunrise.*

Did You Remember to Say Your Prayers Today?

Did You Remember to say your Prayers today?

Did you remember to say your prayers today?
And give thanks to God for the things He has done for you along the way.
For if it were not for the Lord on our side, we would not be here.
His loving presence is all around us and we have nothing to fear.

Because God provides for all our needs according to His riches and glory in Christ Jesus.
We will be able to tell our story of what the Lord has done for us.
And declare, what a mighty God we serve today,
For He is faithful and is with us each day.

And He sees everything and hears us when we pray.
He is everywhere and with us every step of the way.
God loves us and forgives us of all our sin,
And He has a plan for our life that will bring us to
our expected end.

Isaiah 6:24 (KJV) *It shall come to pass That before they call, I will answer; And while they are still speaking, I will hear.*

Forgiving One Another

Forgiving One Another

Forgiving one another helps us to release anger,
Gets rid of hate in your heart and brings you closer together,
Helps you get rest and sleep good at night,
Knowing that you are doing things God's,
way and walking in His divine light.

Because an unforgiving heart can only hurt you,
And it can make you sick and not enjoy the things
you like to do,
But when you forgive one another, you will have
peace of mind,
And Jesus will forgive you of your sins so you can move
forward in time.

Life is so much better when you speak kind words to each other.
You will be filled with joy and love for one another.
You will enjoy life to the fullest if you forgive,
And when you forgive yourself, you will be free to receive the many blessings God has to give.

To God be the Glory!

Matthew 18:21-22 (KJV) *Then came Peter to him, and said, Lord, how oft shall my brother sin against me, and I forgive him? till seven times? Jesus saith unto him, I say not unto thee, Until seven times: but, Until seventy times seven.*

God Loves a Cheerful Giver

God loves a Cheerful Giver

You know God loves a cheerful giver
When you give of your first fruits to the Father
He will bless you and your love ones beyond measure
And He will find favor in you and take much pleasure

When you give your best to God, He will reward you
He is glorified and your life will be changed and made new
He will protect you both day and night
And you will walk in His glorious light

Giving is another way of saying thank you, God
It shows a desire to please the Father and your faith
in His Holy Word

Never hold back on giving to God because He is the main source
And He gives us the opportunity to make the right choice.

2 Corinthians 9:7 (KJV) *Every man according as He purposeth in His heart, so let Him give; not grudgingly, or of necessity: for God loveth a cheerful giver.*

Keep Your Eyes on the Prize

Keep Your Eyes on the Prize

Some people think money can buy you everything.
But without God, you can do nothing
He is the one who makes your dreams come true
He will pick you up when you're down and is always there for you.

So don't put your hope on material things,
Or earthly treasures, not even your friends.
Only trust in God for He is your main source
and provider.
He will heal all of your sickness and disease
like no other.

And when the storms of life come your way
Always remember God is with you every day.
You may even feel like giving up
But just keep pressing on, no matter what.

For your ship will soon come in one day
So don't miss out and let it slip away
Always keep your eyes on the prize
And one day, your heavenly Father will reward you with a big surprise.

Matthew 6:33 (KJV) *Seek ye first the Kingdom of God and His righteousness and all of these things shall be added unto you.*

I ♥ MY HUSBAND

I Love My Husband

I love my husband because He makes me laugh and smile.
I like to see him dress up in the latest styles.
I love when He holds me tight and kisses me good night.
Which brings me joy and delight.

His eyes are a reflection of God's love.
I knew He was sent from heaven above.
He makes me feel so proud to be His wife,
and stand by Him no matter what happens in life.

I like to see and hear Him sing songs of praise,
While others watch and listen in amaze.
He loves to see children laugh and play,
And He asks God to bless them along the way.

I thank God for my husband, Calvin for being my best friend.
Someone that I can count on and depend.
I love my husband because He is gentle to hold,
But most of all because He has a heart of gold.

From: Your Loving Wife, Anita

Let No Man Put Asunder

Let No Man Put Asunder

When God joins a man and woman together
Let no man put asunder,
He blesses the marriage to love one another,
And to always encourage each other.

He desires them to love and not hate,
And to always cherish each other and to mostly appreciate
God's gift from heaven sent from above,
And His blessings are filled with love.

No matter what you're going through in life,
He will bring you out of bondage and strife,
Just call on the name of Jesus, morning, noon
and night,
And everything will be alright.

Matthew 19:6 (KJV) *Wherefore they are no more twain, but one flesh. What therefore God hath joined together, let not man put asunder.*

Thank You, Mom

Thank you, Mom

Thank you, Mom for your love
You are a blessing from heaven above
And you were always there to reason,
No matter what time of the season.

You sent me to school with my brothers each day,
Packed our lunch bags and checked on us every day.
You made sure we went to church together,
And you washed and cooked for us like no other.

Even though you had to work every day,
You went over our homework and always told us before
going to bed at night to pray.
I thank God for your love and dedication,
And making sure, we get a good education.

I can remember when you had to work at night,
And how Dad came to get you with a smile so bright.
Though you both worked hard and for a long time,
You both lived to retire and enjoy life and some sunshine.

Memories of you will always be dear to my heart,
As a loving Mom, you are so wise and smart.
I thank God for blessing me to have a Mom like you,
Someone that I could talk to and do the things that you do.

Proverbs 31:10 (NKJV) *Who can find a virtuous woman? For her price is far above rubies.*

From: Your loving daughter, Anita

While Waiting Patiently for God

While Waiting Patiently for God

As I sit waiting patiently for God each day
I knew a change was going to come my way.
We were joined together in Holy Matrimony,
As man and wife, we lived in peace and harmony.

Our marriage was made in heaven to last,
And even though time passes by so fast,
I remember opening my eyes to see,
My darling, you were still always there for me.

I began to thank God for His goodness and mercy,
He kept us together so we can live to see,
And be thankful for His love and kindness,
For He has saved us, and we will always serve Him for the rest of our days with great joy and gladness.

Psalm 121:1-2 (KJV) *I will lift up mine eyes unto the hills, from whence cometh my help. My help cometh from the Lord, which made heaven and earth.*

God Always Has a Ram in the Bush

God Always Has a Ram in the Bush

Sometimes you do not know who is going to help you,
It may be a child, or someone sent out of the blue,
But you know, 'God always has a Ram in the Bush'
So, you do not have to fret or worry about anything,
or be discouraged and in a big hurry over nothing.

He is always on time and will come through,
And He will never leave or forsake you.
God is love and His word is so powerful,
And He keeps His promises and is faithful.

So, always trust in God and never give up!
He will take you through no matter what.
Though storms may come, and winds may blow,
His power and might is for all to see and know.

Colossians 1:27 (KJV) *Christ in you, the Hope of Glory.*

My Sheep Hear My Voice

My Sheep Hear My Voice

My sheep hear my voice and I know them
And they will listen and follow Me
I will give them peace and serenity,
And a heavenly place for all eternity

As time passes by and seasons change,
Winds may blow, think it not strange?
My people will know Me when I call
Though they may stumble, they will not fall.

Instead, they will come close and draw near
Now open your heart and your ears to hear
And receive what God has for you.
He will make all your dreams come true.

John 10:27-28 *My sheep hear my voice, and I know them, and they will follow me. And I give unto them eternal life; and they shall never perish, neither shall any man pluck them out of my hand.*

Who Do You Say That I AM?

Who Do You Say That I AM?

You are the Rose of Sharon
and God's only begotten Son
You are the Prince of Peace,
The Lilly of the Valley and
The bright and morning star
Your light shines no matter how far.

You are the living waters, and your name is Jesus,
Emmanuel, God is with us
You are my Lord and Savior
All praise belongs to You, and I give you all the glory and honor.

You are the most-high King
And in my heart, You will always reign
But most of all, You are Christ,
The Son of the Living God. Amen

Matthew 16:13-16 (KJV) *When Jesus came into the coasts of Caesarea Philippi, He asked His disciples saying Whom do men say that I the Son of Man am? And they said, some say that thou are John the Baptist: some, Elias, and others, Jeremias, or one of the prophets, He saith unto them, But who say ye that I am? And Simon Peter answered and said, Thou art the Christ, the Son of the living God.*

God Answers Prayers

God Answers Prayers

One morning while I was looking outside my window
I thought about how the Lord is on high, but He looks down low,
Then I noticed that there were not too many people around
Yet, winter had passed away and there was no snow on the ground
To my surprise, mostly all the stores were all shut down.
At first, I thought I was dreaming because it looked like a deserted town.

Everyone was being quarantined at home, both young and old,
And as the pandemic grew out of control, the news began to unfold.
Many people became sick and were leaving this world almost every day.
As I prayed to God, and I believed that help is on the way.

The Lord already knew coronavirus would spread everywhere,
And sooner or later, it was going to show up at our doorstep, but He did not give us a spirit of fear.
This was a time to come together at home.
So, we can be closer together and to love our family and not feel alone.

God really has a message for the whole world to see,
And that is, you can't survive or do anything without Me.
The Lord will supply all of our needs according to His riches in Glory by Christ Jesus,

And despite of what it looks like, God answers prayers and can heal us from anything including coronavirus.

Matthew 19:26 (KJV) *With men this is impossible; but with God all things are possible.*

Spiritual Gift of Wisdom

Spiritual Gift of Wisdom

The spiritual gift of wisdom can be yours today
It is the highest gift of the holy spirit and guides you along the way
It helps you to make the right decision
Giving you spiritual insight and a clearer vision

It's a gift from God and is opened to anyone
But is available to everyone
It doesn't matter if you are not able to walk or run
Or if you are male or female

This spiritual gift gives you knowledge and understanding
And an ability to judge and have wise thinking
All it requires is that you ask God when you pray
Just believe and receive your gift of wisdom and don't delay.

1 Kings 3:9-12 *Solomon asked for: an understanding heart, discernment, and wisdom. The Lord was pleased and gave Solomon wisdom, but He also gave Him what He didn't ask for: long life, riches, and success in battle. No one before or after has been as wise as Solomon …*

Victory in Jesus

Victory in Jesus

What a blessing to live and to be free
But we must never take it for granted,
How God has won the victory,
Or those that fought for this country,
So that we can have peace and liberty.

God has bought us from a mighty long way,
If it was not for the Lord, we would not be here today.
Sometimes, He may not always come when you want Him,
But He is always right on-time.

He has fought so many battles for us,
And sent us His only begotten Son, Jesus,
To stand along by our side
And always there to guide,

All you have to do is love one another,
Trust and obey our Heavenly Father.
Jesus has already paid the price,
And where the Spirit of the Lord is,
there is liberty and Victory in Jesus!

1 Corinthians 15:57 (KJV) *But thanks be to God, which giveth us the victory through our Lord Jesus Christ*

Nobody Knows the Hour or Day

Nobody Knows the Day or Hour

One day, a Virgin Mary was with child, and she gave birth,
It was like Heaven came down to earth,
All the Angels in heaven rejoiced and sang
Glory to the newborn King!

His name shall be called Jesus,
Wonderful, Counselor, Prince of Peace
Thank God for His love and grace,
And for His mercy upon us.

Heaven and earth shall pass away,
But God's word will always stay.
He will come back again someday,
But no man knows the day or hour,
Only the Father who has all the power.

Matthew 24:36 (KJV) *But of that day and hour knoweth no man, no, not the angels of heaven, but my Father only.*

Don't Wait for Tomorrow

Don't Wait for Tomorrow

There is a spiritual warfare going on every day
And we must always be vigilant and pray
We must keep our faith and trust in the Lord,
Always obey and live according to His Holy Word.

We must walk in brotherly love with one another,
Until we are called home to be with our Father.
Jesus is going to come back again,
And He will take His people to heaven with Him.

Jesus will rule over rulers as Lord and King,
And He will sit on the throne of David to reign.
Now is the time to get ready and do not wait,
For tomorrow might be too late.

Revelation 1:7 (ESV) *Behold, He is coming with the clouds, and every eye will see him, even those who pierced him, and all tribes of the earth will wail on account of him. Even so. Amen.*

Joy Cometh in the Morning

Joy Cometh in the Morning

O Lord bless Your people and restore our land
Each day as we live, take us by the hand
Help us always to love and not hate each other
Remembering to forgive and not hurt one another.

Bless this whole world and restore our family
Bring them back together to worship You only
Create in us a pure and clean heart,
So that we can live together and never be apart.

Lord bless the little children to follow You
Help us to train and teach them what to do
Because they are our future generation
They may be called to speak to the nation.

When we pray and give thanks everyday
Lord watch and protect us along the way.
Help us to always trust in You Lord,
And to live according to Your Holy Word.

Even while there maybe some days of sorrow
Give us hope and courage to face tomorrow.

Psalm 30:5 (KJV) *Weeping may endure for a night, but joy cometh in the morning.*

Journal

Testimony I: How My Wife and I Met Each Other

On September 30, 1990, I was on my way to play tennis at a park called Bradbury. I was on the street getting ready to make a left turn at the light but thought about needing some breakfast so I would have enough energy to play my game. So, at the last second, I drove straight up the street to the McDonald's on Silver Hill Road in Suitland, Maryland.

I ordered my food at the drive-thru window and parked in one of the parking spaces. Then I noticed this lady drive up next to me in a Ford Escort and parked. I also noticed she had ordered her breakfast at the drive-thru as well. Now previously, I had been praying to God to meet the right lady for me and to keep from making a mistake, I asked that He show me a sign. Well after seeing I ordered breakfast and she ordered breakfast. I parked and she parked next to me. I said, "Lord, this must be your sign that she is the one."

Looking over at her, I said to myself, "she looks nice and wondered how I could say something to her without being too forward." So, I took my watch off hoping she didn't see me with it on, pointing to my arm and said, "Excuse me, Ma'am but do you have the time? She gave me the time and did not say anything corny like, it's time for you to get a watch. I liked the way she gave me the time and that opened the door for a conversation.

I introduced myself by saying, my name is Calvin and what is your name? She said, "It is Anita." We talked about what brought us to McDonald's. I told her about my last-minute stop for breakfast before going to play tennis and she told me about having her car repaired at the Good Year up the street. She said the Manager told her, it would be a while before getting to her car, so she should go get something to eat and come back. I finally ask Anita for her phone number, and she would not give it to me but asked for my phone number. She said, "I may call you later on."

She called me and I'm glad she did. We talked and decided to meet at the Pizza Hut in Marlow Heights for dinner and had a good time. Anita told me that evening that she had also been praying to God to meet someone for quite some time. She said, "the Holy Spirit told her that same morning that she may just meet a nice person today." We were happy that our steps were ordered by God and because of our meeting at McDonald's, we developed a relationship and got married the next year and are happily married today.

    To God Be the Glory! God answers prayers.

Testimony II: The Day of our 15th Year Wedding Anniversary

On March 7, 2006, my wife and I went out to celebrate our 15th Wedding Anniversary. We had dinner at Topolino restaurant that night and really enjoyed the evening out. After we finished our meal, I told my wife that I would take care of the bill by paying with cash. She told me to pay by credit card because her parents always taught her to keep some money on her just in case of an emergency. But I insisted on paying the bill with cash because it was our Anniversary.

So, I did, and we left the restaurant returning home. I parked our vehicle right in front of our townhouse and got out. I stepped up on the sidewalk and noticed three young men with hoodies coming toward me. I spoke to them asking them how they were doing, and they barely spoke as I was attempting to walk around to get my wife out of the vehicle. Then one of the young men pointed a gun to my head. He said to give him all my money. And the first thing I thought of was that I did not have any money on me because I had spent it all on our Wedding Anniversary meal. I told him that I did not have any money on me but that my wife would give him money. I could see my wife sitting in our vehicle shocked and watching what was happening to me. I told my wife to give him all the money she had. The young man told one of the guys that was with him to go and get the money.

I was praying to God, as he held the gun to my head, that we would not be harmed during the robbery. After getting the money, the young man told me to give him my keys I had in my hand because I did not need them. I did and he told me to lie face down on the sidewalk and instructed my wife to get out of the vehicle and do the same. Then the three young men jumped into our vehicle and drove off. We were so relieved and thankful to be alive, we cared nothing about our vehicle, just that they took themselves away from us.

We got up from the sidewalk and called the police telling them we had just been robbed. We needed shelter so we went to our neighbor's house telling her what happened and waited for the police to arrive. They took a report from us, and we stayed at our neighbor's house until my wife's brother picked us up taking us to my mother-in-law's house.

We got our vehicle back within two weeks. It was not damaged but the police had to do their investigation by placing powder inside checking for fingerprints. We had our bible on the back seat of the vehicle, and it was still there when we got it back. So, God was with us the entire time.

Romans 8:31 (KJV) *If God be for us, who can be against us.*

Note: It is important to believe in God and that He will protect you and to listen to your wife. She did tell me not to pay the bill with cash just in case there was an emergency.

God is our Savior!

Testimony III: The Night Our Townhouse Caught on Fire

On Wednesday, August 24, 2011, it was a day that we will never forget. My husband, Calvin and I got up early for work, that morning and I can remember him asking me, "Are you going to church tonight for Bible Study?" And, I said, "No, I don't think so especially after the earthquake the day before which was felt throughout the D.C., Maryland, Virginia (DMV) area. All I wanted to do was to go straight home and get some rest.

In the meantime, while we were getting ready for work that morning, I noticed the bedroom door move slightly. Then I started thinking that the Lord was trying to tell me something and to see what I was going to do. In other words, was I going to stay home or go to Bible Study? Then I told my husband that I changed my mind, I'm going with him to Bible Study tonight because I want to praise God and thank Him for saving us.

Later, that night after work, we went to Bible Study and our Pastors/Apostles Tony and Cynthia Brazelton were teaching on 'Ways to Strengthen Yourself in the Lord." Before the church service ended, we received a text message from one of our neighbors letting us know it was an 'Emergency' at our townhouse and to come home right away. Then another one of our neighbors called and said that "Our house was on fire," and I started thinking that I must have left a lamp on in the house that overheated. While driving home, we prayed and asked God that everything would be alright. We received another call for us to park our vehicle at the Recreation Center up the street from our townhouse because we would not be able to drive but we'd have to walk back due to the entrance being blocked off by fire equipment.

After arriving at the Recreation center nearby where we lived, we saw the fire was still burning and how it had spread over to another neighbor's house. There were fire trucks on the scene and lots of people including our neighbors and the news media watching the fire.

Our neighbors were so happy to see that we were okay. They thought one of us was inside the house because one of our vehicles that we normally would drive to church was parked out front. While watching the fire, another one of our neighbors asked us, "Where were you all before the fire started?" And we said, "We were at bible study.

Later on, we found out from our Insurance Company that the fire started from our next-door neighbor smoking in bed and that the firefighters had to kick in our front door because they couldn't get an answer. This was a fast-moving fire and a windy night, but the good news is that there were no fatalities with the exception of our next-door neighbor's dog. Before this fire, we had just purchased some new furniture and started renovating our townhouse. But we realized that the most important thing was that we could get another house and furniture, but we could not get another life.

We were so thankful that we were at church that night and in the right place at the right time. Halleluiah! Glory To God!

According to Psalm 46:1 (KJV) it says, *"You are our refuge and strength, a very present help in trouble."* We knew that insurance was important but if it weren't for God on our side, things could have easily gone the other way.

On that same night of the fire, my husband, Calvin and I had to find a place to stay. The Red Cross offered to place us in the Holiday Inn Express hotel in Camp Springs, Maryland for two nights and we stayed one night at the Old Country Suites.

Later on, we were able to go back into our house to retrieve some important documents that were not damaged. The insurance company moved us into a nice and convenient place called Chelsea West which was located within walking distance to Branch Avenue Metro Station. We stayed there for eight months until our townhouse was completely renovated. After going by to see our newly renovated home, which was fixed up so nicely, we almost decided to move back in but we decided that we preferred a single-family home that was not attached.

Then one weekend, we went out looking for a single-family home and God blessed us to find a house. We put in the paperwork, was approved and moved into a new and better house on January 8, 2012, while waiting for our townhouse to sell. During this time, a close friend of the family recommended a friend that she knew who was into Real Estate to help us sell our townhouse. By April 15, 2012, our townhouse went on the market. We prayed to God to help us sell our townhouse. Exactly one year later, our townhouse was sold to a nice young man, and we were relieved from having to pay two mortgages. Halleluiah! Glory to God!

Joel 2:25 (KJV) *And I will restore to you the years that the locust hath eaten, the cankerworm, and the caterpillar, and the palmerworm, my great army which I sent among you.*

We thank God, our Pastors/Apostles Tony & Cynthia Brazelton, all of the Elders and for all those who prayed for us especially during this time.

James 5:16 (KJV) *The effectual fervent prayers of the righteous man availeth much.*

Colossians 1:27 (KJV) *Christ in you, the hope of glory.*

About Calvin Boone

Calvin Boone is a Deacon at Victory Christian Ministries International (VCMI) church.

He was born to the parents of Geneva and Lee Ernest Boone in Newport News, VA in 1953 and was raised in Conway, NC. To know Calvin is to experience His keen sense of humor, spirit of laughter and love of people. He has a passion for working with the homeless, elderly and serving His community. He also enjoys singing praises to God.

He is a faithful husband, father of two children, Tonia and Stacy and four grandchildren Princess, PJ, Alex and JR. He has been married for thirty years to His wife, Anita Boone. Currently, Calvin resides in Southern Maryland, and he served in the Drama Ministry as a Minister of Drama and received the Catch Award in 2011 for His faithfulness. He is a member of the Mighty Men of Valor (MMOV) and Fishers of Men (FOM). His work history includes the former Greater Southeast Community Hospital where He worked most of his eight years as an Orderly in the Operating Room. He also worked at Electronic Data Systems (EDS) for eleven years as a Private Security Officer and Business Analyst. His last place of employment was with the Federal Trade Commission (FTC) as an Administrative Support Assistant in the Director's Office, and after 19 years of Federal Government service, he retired and received a Meritorious Award in 2016. He is also a Veteran of the United States Army.

Calvin is the author of the book entitled *See Right Here Poems* which is a book of inspirational poems.

He enjoys playing and watching tennis, basketball and baseball. His favorite baseball teams are the New York Yankees and the Washington Nationals. His favorite tennis players are Serena and Venus Williams and Roger Federer. He also likes watching his favorite team the Washington Football Team formerly known as the Washington Redskins but His Heavenly Father is Jesus Christ and without Him, none of the above would be possible.

Calvin's Acknowledgements

We want to take this time to thank God for blessing, healing and keeping us. We give Him all the Praise, all the Glory, all the Honor and inspiration for being able to write **2gether Do-N-Poetry with God is Poetic,** To God Be the Glory. Also, we like to thank our Pastors/Apostles Tony and Cynthia Brazelton for being such good role models of God. We thank them for praying for our marriage and thank God for being married for 30 years and more to come.

James 5:16 (KJV) *The effectual fervent prayer of a righteous man availeth much.*

To our very good friends Sharon and Dave, Sharon's mother Joan (deceased), Cousin Betty, Ministers Claire and John, we can never thank you enough for your love and support.

To the Deacon Ministry, Fishers of Men (FOM) and Mighty Men of Valor (MMOV) and Virtual Life Groups, much love to all of you. We thank Minister LaKesha of The Vision to Fruition Publishing House for her help in bringing our book to a completion in Jesus Name, Amen.

May God bless our family and friends and anyone that we have failed to mention, while in the pursuit of our goal.

To God Be the Glory!

About Anita Boone

Anita Boone is a Deacon and serves as one of the Altar Leads at Victory Christian Ministries International (VCMI) church.

Lois Anita Taylor was born to Thomas Ulysses and Virginia Louise Taylor in the District of Columbia in 1950 at Georgetown Hospital. Her family refers to her as Lois, but she goes by Anita.

To know Anita is to experience her loving, patient and warm spirit. She has a passion for working with the homeless, elderly, and serving her community.

Anita is a faithful wife, mother of two bonus daughters, Tonia and Stacy and four grandchildren: Princess, PJ, Alex, and J.R. She has been married to Calvin Boone for thirty years. And currently resides in Southern Maryland. Her work history includes working at the United States Department of State as Management Analyst in Records Management and Program Analyst. Her last place of employment was working in the Department as a Lead Program Analyst/Government Information Specialist for the Freedom of Information Act and Privacy Act programs in the Office of Management and Public Diplomacy (MPD). Upon occasion, she would serve as Acting

Branch Chief. She has also worked at other federal agencies throughout her career. After 43 years of United States Government service, she retired and received the Expeditionary Service Global Award, the United States flag, and the Secretary's Career Achievement Award in 2016.

Anita graduated from Eastern High School with honors and received a BA degree in Political Science and minor in Sociology from Dunbarton College of Holy Cross in 1973. She also attended Trinity College majoring in Special Education. She worked as a schoolteacher for the Young, Gifted, and Talented. Her favorite color is royal blue. She attends many of the Virtuous Women's Conferences at Victory Christian Ministries International (VCMI) church and is a member of the Fishers of Men (FOM).

Anita is the author of a bestselling book of inspirational poems entitled *Jesus is the Way.*

Anita enjoys reading, watching tennis and religious movies and listening to gospel music. One of her favorite songs is *"I Never Knew Love Like This Before"*, *"He's Intentional"*, *"Center of My Joy"* and *"Break every Chain"*. Her favorite Christian movie is *"Jesus of Nazareth."*

Anita's Acknowledgements

First of all, we like to take this time to thank our God for blessing, healing and keeping our marriage together. I give Him all the Praise, all the Glory, all the Honor and inspiration for being able to write *2gether Do-N-Poetry with God is Poetic.* We like to thank our Pastors/Apostles Tony and Cynthia Brazelton for praying for us, not only for our marriage but for our family. We like to thank all the Elders and Deacons for your prayers, love and support. we especially like to thank God for being married for 30 years and more to come.

Matthew 18:20 (KJV) *For where two or three are gathered together in my name, there am I in the midst of them.*

To our very good friends Sharon and Dave, Ministers Claire and John, former co-workers, Joyce and Nanette, and former supervisor, Pastor Melody Adams, we can never thank you enough for your love, prayers, and support.

To the Deacon Ministry, Fishers of Men (FOM), Virtuous Women Ministry and Virtual Life Groups, much love to all of you. We thank Minister LaKesha of The Vision to Fruition Publishing House for her help in bringing our book to completion in Jesus Name, Amen.

May God bless our family and friends and anyone that we have failed to mention, while in the pursuit of our goal.

Christ in you, the hope of glory.
Colossians 1:27 (KJV)

About the Publisher

At The Vision to Fruition Group, we are dedicated to helping others bring their personal, business, ministry, and other visions to fruition. Whether your vision is a book you want to write, a business you want to start, a conference or event you want to host, a ministry you want to launch or an organization you want to start; or requires a more technical aspect like computer repairs, logo designs or web designs; we can help. The Vision to Fruition Publishing House is the publishing branch of The Vision to Fruition Group. We will help you walk through the process and set you up for success!

At The Vision to Fruition Group, we have more than just clients, we have Visionaries. We provide solutions to equip others to pursue their visions and dreams with reckless abandon. Since 2017, we have published over 40 authors, several of which were Amazon Bestsellers. We would love for you to join our family of Visionaries as well!

Learn more here: www.vision-fruition.com

Or

www.vtfpublishing.com

www.ingramcontent.com/pod-product-compliance
Lightning Source LLC
Chambersburg PA
CBHW070457090426
42735CB00012B/2594